FINDING
Calm
IN NATURE

-›❧‹-

A GUIDE FOR MINDFUL KIDS

BY JENNIFER GRANT   ILLUSTRATED BY ERIN BROWN

beaming ✹ books
MINNEAPOLIS

Text copyright © 2023 Jennifer Grant
Illustrations by Erin Brown, copyright © 2023 Beaming Books

29 28 27 26 25 24 23   1 2 3 4 5 6 7 8

Hardcover ISBN: 978-1-5064-8513-3
eBook ISBN: 978-1-5064-8514-0

Library of Congress Cataloging-in-Publication Data

Names: Grant, Jennifer (Jennifer C.), author. | Brown, Erin (Illustrator),
   illustrator.
Title: Finding calm in nature : a guide for mindful kids / by Jennifer
   Grant ; illustrated by Erin Brown.
Description: Minneapolis, MN : Beaming Books, 2023. | Audience: Ages 9-12 |
   Summary: "A guide to help kids process their big feelings with soothing
   descriptions of nature and mindfulness prompts"-- Provided by publisher.

Identifiers: LCCN 2022023126 (print) | LCCN 2022023127 (ebook) | ISBN
   9781506485133 (hardcover) | ISBN 9781506485140 (ebook)
Subjects: LCSH: Nature--Psychological aspects--Juvenile literature. | Human
   ecology--Psychological aspects--Juvenile literature. | Mindfulness
   (Psychology)--Juvenile literature.
Classification: LCC BF353.5.N37 G73 2023 (print) | LCC BF353.5.N37
   (ebook) | DDC 155.9/1--dc23/eng/20220523
LC record available at https://lccn.loc.gov/2022023126
LC ebook record available at https://lccn.loc.gov/2022023127

VN0004589; 9781506485133; JAN2023

Beaming Books
PO Box 1209
Minneapolis, MN 55440-1209
Beamingbooks.com

FOR **CLAYTON, SAMUEL, AND MARINA LYNN**

MAY YOU CONTINUE TO FIND CALM—
AND JOY!—IN NATURE. —JG

HAPPINESS, KNOWLEDGE, NOT IN
ANOTHER PLACE BUT THIS PLACE,
NOT FOR ANOTHER HOUR
BUT THIS HOUR.

— Walt Whitman
"A SONG FOR OCCUPATIONS"

CONTENTS

I CAN START FRESH

IN THE BEGINNER'S MIND THERE ARE MANY POSSIBILITIES; IN THE EXPERT'S MIND THERE ARE FEW.

—Shunryu Suzuki

A plant begins life as a seed, buried underground, invisible. Then, at just the right moment, the seed sprouts and breaks out of the outer shell. Roots grow, and then the seedling rises up through the dirt, stretching and reaching for the open air to find sunlight and room to bloom.

Like a sunflower standing beside a wooden fence or like pumpkins growing in garden patches, people need sun, air, and water to live. We also start small and change in surprising ways as we grow up. And like plants, there are so *many* different kinds of us! One person might be like a pine tree, tall and quiet in the woods. Another is like a pink water lily, showy and sweet smelling, lighting up the surface of a lake.

And like sturdy dandelions poking up through cracks in the sidewalk, sometimes people live in places that feel as hard and jagged as a block of concrete. We go through times when we don't know what is happening or how long it will be before we feel happy again. We break out of our shells, we grow our roots, and we are stretched during these hard times. We change. And change can feel very uncomfortable—and sometimes even painful.

One way to feel better when we are hurting is to spend time outside in nature. Being outdoors is good for our bodies and our minds. In Japan doctors sometimes give patients prescriptions for walks in the forest, just like another doctor might tell you to take vitamins to stay healthy or give you antibiotics or other medicine to recover from being sick. Being outdoors in nature helps our bodies stay healthy, helps us heal more quickly when we are sick or injured, and often cheers us up.

It especially calms us down to look at the earth and sky—and also the "nature" we find indoors, like pets and potted plants—with what is called a "beginner's mind."

Being a beginner is about starting fresh.

Think about a time when you were a beginner and saw or did something for the first time. Maybe you remember the first time you sat down at a piano or the first time you put on a baseball glove or the first time you picked up a paintbrush. You were a beginner then—and like all beginners, you probably felt curious, not sure what would happen next, and very focused. You had a beginner's mind; you were starting fresh.

Part of the fun of spending time with babies and really little kids is that they look at the world with fresh eyes. There are so many things they do, see, touch, taste, and feel for the very first time.

Watch a baby play with their shadow sometime. Babies usually start noticing shadows when they are about seven or eight months old. They lift up their hands, and the shadow moves. *What in the world?* they seem to be thinking.

A few months later, they start using their fingers as "pinchers" to try different foods, like little pieces of cereal or cut-up grapes. When they first put a new kind of food into their mouths, they are curious, they don't yet know what it will taste like, and they are very, very focused on what's happening right then. *Will this be sweet? Sour? Will it be crunchy or soft? Will I like it?* They don't know yet! There are a million possibilities!

Although you already know what a grape tastes like, and you already know that a shadow is formed when something gets in the way of the light, you can still practice beginner's mind.

Looking at the world with fresh eyes is soothing. It calms us down to watch a tree standing in stillness, see the breeze make ripples on a puddle, and stare up at the clouds. Seeing all of this beauty, with that open beginner's mind, can help us let go of difficult or painful thoughts and feelings.

Nature is a kind teacher and friend. Nature reminds us that the world is full of endless possibilities and charms us with stunning shows of color. The natural world entertains us with designs and sounds and wonders of all kinds. Nature reminds us that seeds become plants, that things can look one way one day and look another way the next, and that spring always, finally, comes—even after the longest, coldest winter.

Nature is always beginning again, always starting fresh.

Go outside and let nature be your teacher and friend when your feelings are tangled up in knots or when you need a break from what's troubling you on the inside. And remember that like a plant or flower, you are strong and beautiful and you will sprout, grow, stretch, and bloom at just the right time.

PRACTICING BEGINNER'S MIND
TRY EXPLORING SOMETHING LIKE A BEGINNER:

1. Find one thing you've had for a long time. It could be a toy, book, backpack, or anything else.

2. Decide to look at it as if you've never seen it before. Maybe say in your mind, "Hmmm . . . what is this?"

3. If you were from another planet and had never seen this before, what would you think this thing was for? What are some ways you could use it or play with it or wear it that you've never tried?

4. Don't judge the item as good or bad, old or new, useful or silly. Just quietly look at it. *What color is it? What does it feel like? Does it have a smell? How heavy is it? Is there an underneath or hidden part you can find? Is there anything you are noticing about it that you have never noticed before?*

5. After a minute or two, think about other things or people you know really, really well. Can you look at them with a curious beginner's mind too?

I AM
ROOTED

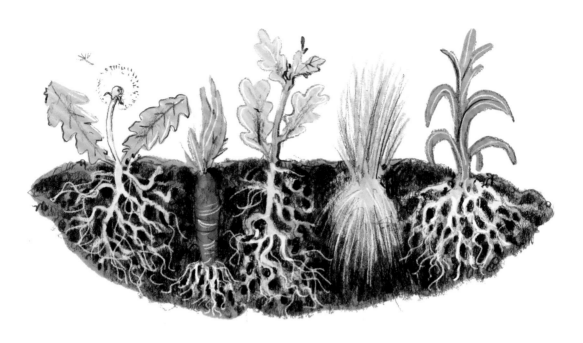

Roots are the underground parts of plants. They have tiny "root hairs" that soak up water and minerals from the soil to keep plants healthy. Roots also help plants stand up straight and not blow over when it's windy or stormy.

When people talk about their "roots," sometimes they are talking about the place where they used to live or faraway places where their grandparents or other people they love now live.

"I live in Chicago," a person might say. "But my roots are in Dallas."

Another way people use the word *roots* to talk about themselves has to do with the things that matter most to them.

"My love of art is rooted in the fact that my mother is a painter," a person could say.

Or you could say, "My love for unicorns is deeply rooted. I've loved them since I was two years old!"

People we love and trust "keep us rooted." When we are going through hard times, these people help us and listen to us. They stay with us. This helps us to be strong, just like the roots of plants feed and support them and keep them strong, even in the harshest storms.

DID YOU KNOW?

There are two main types of root systems in plants:

- The taproot system: one main root goes down into the ground, with smaller roots growing out.
- The diffuse, or fibrous, root system: many roots grow in all directions.

When you eat a carrot, you're actually eating the carrot plant's taproot. Some other plants that have a taproot system are dandelions and trees such as oaks, elms, and pines.

Grass is an example of a plant with a diffuse root system. Corn, rice, wheat, and oats also have this kind of root system.

Most trees do not have a taproot, and their roots can be found in the top 18 inches of soil. Although they don't have deep roots, huge trees can stand tall, even in harsh storms, because their roots spread out and away from them. The roots of a redwood tree can grow outward as far as 100 feet from the tree's trunk.

DID YOU KNOW?

Wild fig trees are thought to have the deepest roots in the world and are found in South Africa. With roots reaching 400 feet, the wild fig's roots are deeper than the Statue of Liberty is tall!

I AM BEAUTIFUL

A famous author and medical doctor named Herbert Benson created a fun and easy way to help his patients calm down. He asked them to choose a word or phrase—or a "mantra"— that was "firmly rooted" in their belief system. Mantras are short, positive statements that people silently repeat that make them feel better and remind them of good things. Examples of mantras include "I am loved," "Everything will work out," "I choose peace," and "I am beautiful." Dr. Benson said that when we let our faces relax and quietly repeat our mantras, our bodies and minds calm down. Next time you are feeling nervous or tense, find a quiet place to sit for a few minutes and try out Dr. Benson's tip! Pick a mantra that roots you!

I AM LOVED

INSIDE OF YOU, THERE IS A PEACE AND REFUGE,
TO WHICH YOU CAN GO AT EVERY HOUR OF
THE DAY AND BE AT HOME AT YOURSELF.

— *Herman Hesse*
SIDDHARTHA

DANDELIONS

MAKING IT THROUGH TOUGH TIMES

Bad things that are happening in our own homes or even very far away in the world can make us feel sad, angry, and confused. Sometimes what's making us feel bad is something private that's really hard to explain.

Every person in the whole world goes through hard times. Sometimes these difficult patches last a minute. Sometimes they last a day or even a week, and sometimes for a much longer time.

When people go through really challenging times, they find ways to cope. Sometimes they just make it through, one day at a time, until things start to get better. Sometimes a doctor gives them medicine to help them feel better. Sometimes they take a break from work or school or their usual activities so they can recover.

But you know what's surprising?

Lots of times we come out of those hard experiences stronger and—believe it or not—even happier than we were before! As awful as the hard times feel while we are in them, they can do something amazing inside of us: they can make us more resilient.

What is "RESILIENCE"?

Resilience is being able to go through hard times and recover from them. When we are resilient, we tap deep into our own strengths, and we also reach out and ask for other people's help. We can grow stronger and calmer from our difficulties, becoming more resilient over time.

What RESILIENCE IS NOT

Being resilient doesn't mean we'll never feel angry, confused, or sad. Everyone gets upset sometimes. Everyone has disappointments, bad days, and other tough times. But the more resilient we are, the more we can think helpful thoughts in those hard times and make good choices about how to handle our feelings. We can remind ourselves that things aren't always bad and that things will get better.

One of the most resilient plants in nature is the dandelion. Dandelions might seem ordinary to you, but actually they are *amazing*. They grow fast, have deep roots, and can survive harsh conditions. They are also beautiful!

Dandelions' roots are thick and grow deep into the ground; they have taproots.

Their roots help other nearby plants and flowers thrive by bringing nutrients up closer to the surface where neighboring plants can use them.

Did you know that *every single part* of the dandelion can be eaten—and not just by songbirds like sparrows and goldfinches but by humans too?

You can make salads out of dandelion leaves and can make tea by boiling their roots, leaves, and flowers. Thousands of years ago, people used dandelions to treat medical problems like stomachaches; some people still do. Dandelions' yellow flowers can make natural dyes, and the sap or "milk" that drips from their stems can be used to make tires, toys, shoes, and other things.

LOOK AT A DANDELION

LOOK, WITH A BEGINNER'S MIND, AT A DANDELION. SEE HOW, AT DIFFERENT POINTS IN ITS LIFE, A DANDELION LOOKS LIKE THE SUN, THE MOON, AND THE STARS.

When in bloom, they're like the sun.

When they've gone to seed, their white puffballs look like the moon.

Those seeds, blown into the air, look like stars in the night sky.

Like the dandelion, sometimes you warm those around you, like the sun does. Sometimes you're quiet and calm like the moon. And sometimes you twinkle and shine like the stars.

You bring beauty into the world.

You are resilient, and your roots are growing deep.

Practice
DANDELION BREATHING

I magine that you are holding a dandelion, one with a full round puffball of seeds. Now, take a deep breath, and when you let it out, imagine that those seeds are your problems and you are blowing them far, far away. Close your eyes and do this three times. Let your shoulders relax, and just breathe out.

- The dandelion flower in bloom is yellow-orange and made up of many tiny flowers called ray florets. Dandelion flowers open at sunrise and close at night.

- You might think the plants get their name, dandelion, because of their yellow "mane," but the name actually comes from the French dent de lion, meaning "tooth of the lion," named for their jagged, spiky leaves.

TO HELP GET THROUGH A HARD TIME:

1. Pause and check in with yourself by quietly asking: "What am I feeling?"
2. Take your time and give a name to your feelings, as best as you can.
   - o   I feel sad that my friend is moving.
   - o   I feel scared about what is happening in the world.
   - o   I feel worried because my dog is sick.
3. Imagine you are holding your feelings gently, like a dandelion stem in your hand.
4. Practice dandelion breathing and imagine blowing your worries or hard feelings out into the air.
5. Tell someone you trust what is at the root of the way you feel.
6. Remind yourself that now isn't forever.

DID YOU KNOW?
WIND BUILDS RESILIENCE

When wind blows on a small seedling, like a just-sprouted tomato plant, it helps the plant create a stronger stem. Each time the wind hits the plant, a chemical is released, and the plant grows stronger. People "harden off" plants, too, by putting them outdoors for short times after starting to grow them inside so they can get used to not only wind but also colder temperatures.

When plants are grown in areas where there is no wind or when they are placed outside without being hardened off, they fall over or break more easily than the ones that experience some wind and cooler weather.

People can be that way too. We can grow stronger and more resilient after going through stormy times.

REDWOOD
TREES

LIVING IN COMMUNITY

Imagine that you are a tree living in a thick forest among many other living things. Imagine yourself surrounded by other trees just like you. They shelter you from storms and shade you from the sun.

Who are
THE TREES IN YOUR HUMAN "FOREST"?

Maybe you're rooted with people in your family, with your teachers or neighbors, or with your friends. These people open the door for you, listen when you tell them what happened at school or at the park, and stand beside you year after year. You grow, and they stay with you. They are kind to you, give you good things to eat, help you when you have trouble figuring something out, and take you where you need to go.

Who **ROOTS YOU?**

Take a few moments to think about the trees in your forest. You could even sketch a forest and label the trees with the names of people who you love and depend on.

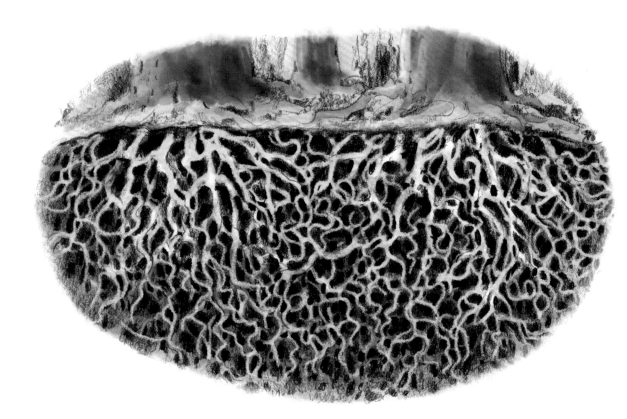

Redwood trees grow in an area about 500 miles long, from the southwestern tip of Oregon down the coast of California. Redwoods are the tallest trees in the world. They are giants, and they can live for hundreds—or even thousands—of years!

Part of the reason redwoods can live so long is their special bark, which is soft, reddish brown, and 6–12 inches thick. This bark protects the trees from forest fires. A fire might scorch the tree's outer bark, but the inside of the tree is kept safe from harm. This thick bark also keeps insects, such as termites, away. The bark on a redwood tree is rough to the touch, but the underside is silky smooth.

Are you surprised to learn that redwood trees, which are hundreds of feet tall, have very shallow roots? Their root systems are sometimes only about 5 or 6 feet deep. Instead of growing a deep taproot, redwood trees spread their shallow roots out over 100 feet and connect with the roots of other trees, forming an interwoven root mass beneath the forest floor.

Redwoods, just like people, live in community and thrive when they support each other.

NO KIND ACTION EVER STOPS WITH ITSELF. ONE KIND ACTION LEADS TO ANOTHER. GOOD EXAMPLE IS FOLLOWED. A SINGLE ACT OF KINDNESS THROWS OUT ROOTS IN ALL DIRECTIONS, AND THE ROOTS SPRING UP AND MAKE NEW TREES. THE GREATEST WORK THAT KINDNESS DOES TO OTHERS IS THAT IT MAKES THEM KIND THEMSELVES.

— Amelia Earhart

Practice
BEING GROUNDED

Imagine that you are standing in front of a massive redwood tree. Picture the tree's roots underground, spreading out far into the silent forest.

Like this tree, you are connected to a web of other living beings. The people in your life support you, and you support them.

You have a sturdy root system that feeds you and helps you to be strong.

Think of one kind thing someone has done for you this week. Breathe in and out, relaxing in that memory.

Think of one kind thing you can do for someone else. Close your eyes and imagine what it feels like when you do this. Imagine the happiness you can give to another person by being kind.

Now stand up where you are, if you can. If you can't, just put your feet down flat on the floor.

Imagine that you are a tree and that your feet are rooted in the earth. Be still for a few moments, knowing that you are like a tree, still and grounded and at peace. Know that you, like the redwood trees, are part of a community.

If you like, you could repeat the words, or mantra, "I am part of something bigger than myself" or "I am not alone" in your mind.

DID YOU KNOW?

The world's largest tree is called "Hyperion." It is a redwood that lives in the Redwood National Park in California. Hyperion is 380 feet tall. Is that hard to picture? Imagine riding along on a highway and a semitruck passes by. The trailers pulled by huge semis are often 53 feet long. So Hyperion is as tall as *more than seven* semitruck trailers are long! Also, at about 600 years old, Hyperion is a rather *young* redwood. They can live to be more than 2,500 years old!

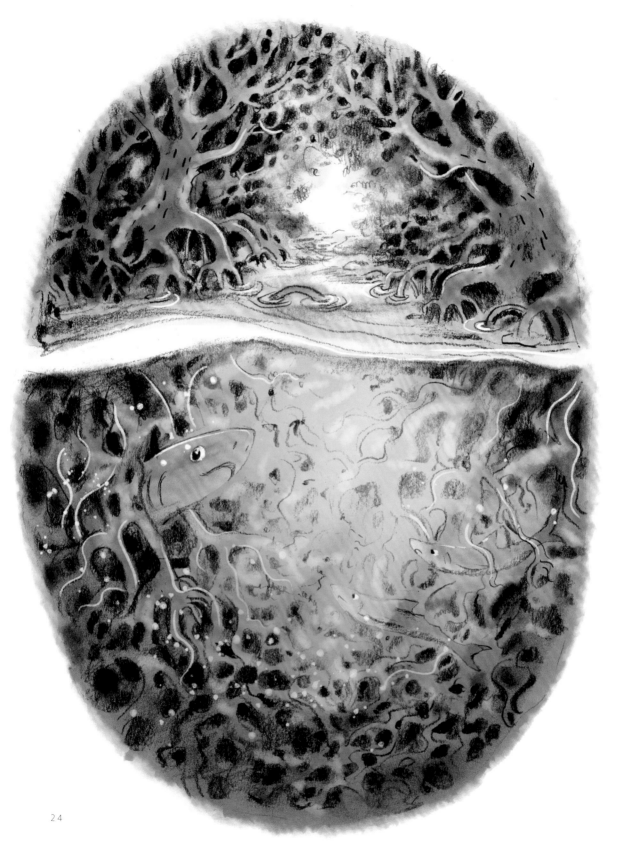

MANGROVE FORESTS

BEING MYSELF

Mangrove trees are different from a lot of other plants and trees, and life isn't easy for them. They don't look like a lot of other trees. They live in places other trees cannot live. And they can do things other trees can't do. They're just plain *different*!

Mangroves live along coastlines where the tide batters and floods their roots. They are also the only trees in the world that can survive on seawater. Saltwater is poison for plants, but mangroves filter out up to 90 percent of the salt found in seawater. They then store the fresh, filtered water in their thick leaves.

We need mangrove trees. Not only do their knotted roots protect the shoreline by keeping the ground in place, but they also guard marine life. Some people call mangrove forests "shark nurseries" because baby sharks (and a lot of other animals too) can safely swim in them, avoiding being hunted by predators out in the open ocean.

Mangroves are also Earth's defenders, capturing and storing carbon dioxide, the gas that causes climate change. Mangrove forests are ten times stronger in fighting global warming than rainforests!

Sometimes you might feel as odd as a mangrove, with jumbled, knotted roots. You might feel like the place you live is too hard, the water too salty, the tides too strong. You might feel different from everyone else.

But like the mangrove, what makes you different makes you needed. This world wouldn't be the same without your unique strength, spirit, and skills.

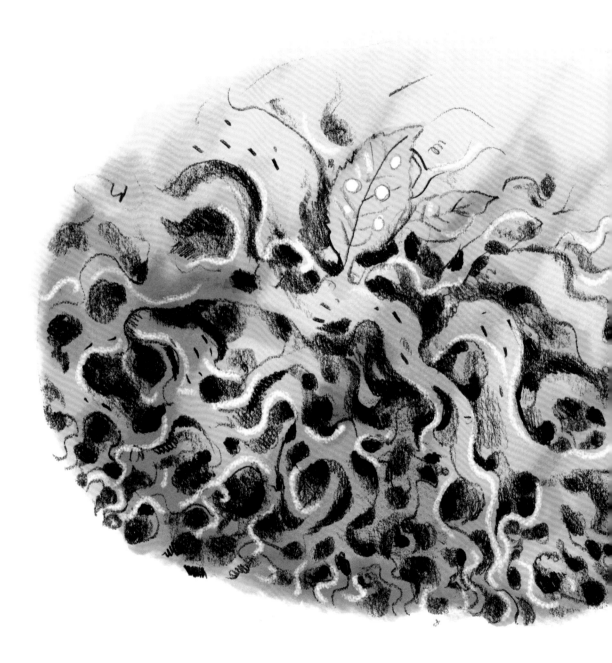

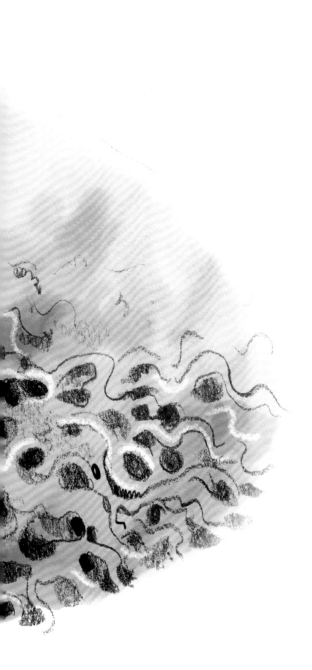

MANGROVES' ROOTS

The root systems of mangrove trees are tangled and thick. They include different types of roots that do different things to help these trees not only survive but *thrive*.

BREATHING ROOTS

Breathing roots are aboveground and—as you may have guessed—help get oxygen from the air into the underground part of the plant. There's sometimes no oxygen at all in the soil where the mangroves grow, so they need to take it in from the surrounding air with their strange-looking breathing roots. Other types of mangrove roots are **stilt roots** that help mangroves stand tall and strong.

What is **OXYGEN?**

The air we breathe contains **oxygen**, which is invisible, tasteless, and odorless—and is all around us and in us. (In fact, 65 percent of a person's body weight is oxygen!) We couldn't live and breathe without it. Neither could other living beings on Earth, like plants and animals.

Practice
A TREE POSE

The "tree pose" position in yoga helps us feel steadier and more balanced.

1. Stand up straight and tall. Take a deep breath.

2. Look ahead and find a point such as a picture on the wall or a piece of furniture across the room to lock your focus on.

3. As you breathe out, slowly bring up your left foot by bending your left knee and lifting your leg. Place your left foot on the inside part of your right leg.

4. Relax and straighten your right leg on the floor and shift your weight to your right foot. Imagine that your right foot and leg are a sturdy taproot, deeply grounded in the earth.

5. Inhale again and bring your hands to your sides. Reach out like branches on a tree. It's okay if you get wobbly, if your left leg needs to drop down onto the floor again. Just start over if you lose balance, breathing deeply in and out.

6. While in the tree pose, bring your hands together in front of your heart and then then lift them over your head like a strong, growing tree.

7. If you like, imagine yourself as a tree. Are you a pine tree? An elm? A cherry tree, all in bloom? Are you a mangrove, with wet, wild roots?

8. Put your left leg down onto the ground again. Take a few even, deep breaths, and now repeat with your right leg.

9. If you like, you can say the words "I am just right, just the way I am" while holding the tree pose.

If you have trouble doing the tree pose, do it another way. If you like to move, pretend you are a tree that is dancing and swaying in the wind or a mangrove dancing in the sea. You could also sit in a chair and stretch out your arms like tree branches, keeping them still or moving them back and forth.

I CAN STRETCH

Sit up tall, extend your arms straight out in front of you, and slowly reach your hands forward as far as they can go. Feel that stretch in your back, shoulders, and upper arms? It feels good, doesn't it?

Often we stretch without even thinking about it, like when we first wake up in the morning or when we stand up after we've been sitting down for a long time.

Other times we stretch on purpose and in a very particular way. If you've ever taken a dance class or played a sport like soccer, your teacher or coach probably guided you through some basic stretches before rehearsal or practice, just so you were "warmed up." Stretching *after* you exercise is important too—it can keep you from getting muscle cramps.

Stretching not only relaxes our bodies **but also** calms our minds. When we slowly stretch, breathing evenly, our heart rates slow down, and we feel a sense of calm.

Animals and other beings in nature stretch too. Birds stretch their wings wide as they fly. Spiders spin their webs and stretch them across tree branches. Dogs and cats stretch their bodies to keep their muscles healthy and to show how they're feeling.

DID YOU KNOW?

There are two main types of stretching: dynamic and static. *Before* doing a fitness activity, dynamic, or moving, stretches are best. Circling your arms and swinging your legs are ways to do this kind of stretching. After physical play, it's best to do a cooldown of **static, or still, stretching**, like slowly bending to touch your toes.

People sometimes use the word "stretch" to mean that something is hard for us.

You might say, "I tried doing my big sister's math homework, but it was too much of a stretch for me."

Or you might use the word when you describe going through a painful time in your life: "My grandma died, and that really *stretched* me."

What has stretched *you*? Missing someone you love? Moving? Being given the chance to do something challenging, like when a teacher or coach pushed you to do your best?

Think of a time when you've felt like you've "stretched your wings" and soared like an eagle. Maybe it was when you played a complicated piece of music well or ran as fast as you could in a race or won at a tricky game like chess or got past a really hard level in a video game.

How did that feel?

Know that, like an eagle, you will find lots of chances to rise up and soar.

Lift

Drag

thrust

weight

WINGSPANS

FEELING LOW AND FINDING LIFT

You've probably watched a bird fly overhead many times. Birds' wings stretch wide, and birds seem to glide up in the sky when they fly. Their bodies are made to fly. They have light, hollow, air-filled bones; beaks instead of heavy jaw-bones and teeth; and sleek body shapes and smooth feathers.

But . . . how do they actually take off and fly? Why doesn't **gravity** pull them down to the ground?

Birds can fly because they resist the force of gravity by using another force called **lift**. Birds create lift by moving through the air with the front part of the wing slightly higher than the back part. Air moves faster over the top of the bird's wing and slower under-neath; the air pressure above the wing is less than the pressure below it, pushing the bird upward. This is how airplanes use lift force to stay up in the air too.

Planes use engines to power them through the atmosphere, but birds stretch their wings to fly. They flap their wings, moving them up and down, to move upward and forward. They push down on their wings to create lift. They can also glide by just extending their wings and letting the air pressure keep them flying. When birds fly high and for long distances, they soar. Soaring is a kind of gliding that makes use of **air currents**.

What is **GRAVITY?**

Gravity is a force of nature that keeps everything pulled down toward the earth. The heavier something is, the stronger the force of gravity.

FEELING DOWN

Sometimes it can feel like a bad mood is pulling our feelings down to the ground, like an invisible force of gravity in our hearts. We can feel angry or lonely or crabby or sad. Maybe we find ourselves crying more often than usual or just feel really tired. Nothing tastes very good. We might not enjoy doing the things we normally like doing. Our favorite books or TV shows or games or people just seem kind of . . . boring and pointless. And instead of mantras that make us feel good, negative words might repeat in our minds—phrases like "I can't do anything right" or "No one likes me."

Doctors call the illness that can cause symptoms like these "depression." Just like when you are sick with an ear infection or the flu, there are things doctors know to do to help you recover from depression.

Doctors do checkups to make sure there isn't a physical reason someone is feeling low. They also might suggest you talk to a "feelings doctor," known as a therapist, who can help you.

When you are feeling sad, it is most helpful to tell a trusted adult that you're feeling that way. Maybe suggest to a parent or relative or other trusted adult that you go together for a walk outside so you can talk about the way you've been feeling. Like many types of birds who flock together—huddling together for warmth and keeping each other safe from predators—people do best when we are connected to others. People who love us want to give us a "lift" when we are having hard feelings or feel like we are stretched too thin.

WHO HAS SEEN THE WIND?

— Christina Rossetti

WHO HAS SEEN THE WIND?
NEITHER I NOR YOU:
BUT WHEN THE LEAVES HANG TREMBLING,
THE WIND IS PASSING THROUGH.

WHO HAS SEEN THE WIND?
NEITHER YOU NOR I:
BUT WHEN THE TREES BOW DOWN THEIR HEADS,
THE WIND IS PASSING BY.

Practice
WINGSPAN STRETCHING

1. Sit or stand with your arms outstretched at your sides, as though you have wings.

2. Turn your thumbs downward, and then move your arms back behind you.

3. Feel the stretch of your back and shoulder blades.

4. Now, slowly turn your thumbs up again and move your arms out to your sides, spreading your "wings."

5. Raise your arms up high, and then straight out from your sides again.

Repeat this a few times.

If you like, you could silently say a mantra such as "I am good enough" or "My feelings matter" or "Things will get better" in your mind.

DID YOU KNOW?

The smallest bird in the world is the bee hummingbird, with a wingspan of just under 2 inches. The bird with the largest wing-span is the wandering albatross, with a wingspan of more than 12 feet. (Picture stacking two refrigerators on top of each other; that would be about 12 feet tall—as long as the wandering albatross's wingspan.)

12 feet

2 inches

SPIDERWEBS

WATCHING ANXIETY FROM A DISTANCE

Have you ever read the book *Charlotte's Web*? It's a story about a pig named Wilbur and his very best friend, a spider who saves his life. In the novel, the spider introduces herself as "Charlotte A. Cavatica."

The **scientific name** of barn spiders is *Araneus cavaticus*, so the author was letting us know exactly what kind of spider Charlotte is. She's part of the genus "Araneus" (meaning orb-weaving spiders) and the species "cavaticus" (from the Latin word that means "living in caves"). The author of *Charlotte's Web* was an American man named E. B. White. White was a very shy and nervous person; he said his anxiety was a disability. Anxiety can make a person feel grumpy or angry, give them trouble sleeping, and make them have headaches or stomachaches. Anxiety can feel other ways too.

When people would knock on E. B. White's office door, sometimes he felt so nervous that he would open the window and go outside to hide on the fire escape.

White felt most comfortable and relaxed when he was outside in nature. He got the idea for his book about Wilbur and Charlotte while outdoors on his own farm, quietly watching his pigs and observing a spider spinning a web, just like Fern, the little girl in his novel, watches Charlotte making webs. White felt peaceful at his farm.

While it can feel calming to watch spiders do their silent, careful work, stretching their spider silk from branch to branch, some people are afraid of spiders. Some people are so afraid of them that even talking about spiders makes their hearts race.

Like Charlotte, anxiety can be a kind of strange and interesting friend. It's actually trying to protect us. For instance, feeling anxious or afraid when a dog barks angrily at you keeps you from rushing up close to it. Your fear is trying to keep you safe. Sometimes, though, our fears get overprotective.

One way to feel less anxious about something is to learn about it and just watch it from a distance, like a scientist studying something. We can talk about what makes us feel nervous (whether that is spiders or barking dogs or being around people we don't know) and decide whether we want to be open to this thing or want to keep a little distance from it. Calmly watching it from a distance can help us sort out our feelings.

By pausing and looking with curiosity about what is making us feel uncomfortable, we can sometimes get enough distance from a bad feeling to let it to break off and float away, like an old spider web in the breeze.

In *Charlotte's Web*, not only can Wilbur and all of the other animals on the farm speak to one another but Charlotte can also write. In order to save her friend from being killed by the farmer and sold for meat, she spins a web and stretches it above the part of the barn where Wilbur lives. She writes messages in her web: "Some Pig" and "Terrific" and "Radiant" and "Humble." The farmer decides that these messages that appear in Charlotte's orb-style webs are miracles and that Wilbur is a special pig. He decides to let him live.

Orb webs, like Charlotte's, are the most familiar ones to most people. They look like a wheel with a spiral center and "spokes" leading from the center to the outer edge of the web.

SCIENTIFIC NAMES
How Do Scientific Names Work?

The first word of a scientific name tells the **genus**, or what *group* of animals or plants (with similar qualities or features) the living being is a part of. These animals share a common ancestor. Zebras, donkeys, and horses, for example, are all part of the same genus. While very different, they are similar in some ways and share a great-great-great-great-grandparent. We always capitalize the first word of a scientific name—the genus name.

The second word of a scientific name is the **species**, or *specific type* of living being. This second word of a scientific name is always lowercase.

Most people use what is called the "common name" when talking about living things, but scientists use more exact terms. So while most of us call Charlotte a barn spider or just a spider, scientists call her *Araneus cavaticus*. (And Wilbur calls her a "true friend.")

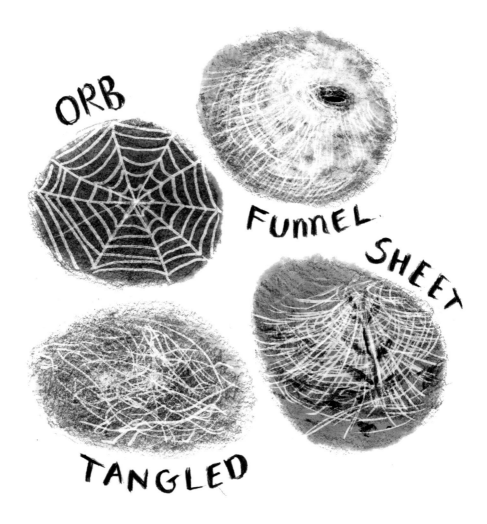

ORB

FUNNEL

SHEET

TANGLED

There are other common types of webs, too, including:

- **Funnel webs:** Narrow in the middle, wider on the sides, funnel webs are usually found low to the ground in wooded areas or places. Spiders use this kind of web as both a trap and a place to hide.

- **Tangled webs:** Often found in attics or basements, these are also called "cobwebs" and do not have regular patterns.

- **Sheet webs:** Looking like a white sheet hanging between trees, in bushes, or on top of grass, sheet webs are very tightly woven.

Practice
OPENING & CLOSING

Sit or stand comfortably. As you take a deep breath in, open your arms, stretching them straight out on either side of you. When you breathe out, wrap your arms around yourself, like you are giving yourself a big hug. Hold your arms around yourself for a few breaths and open your arms up again when you feel ready.

When something or someone makes you feel anxious, you can practice opening and closing up. See what makes you feel safe and comfortable. Open your arms when you feel curious and safe; enclose yourself in a big hug when you want to feel protected.

GIVE YOUR FEAR A SCIENTIFIC NAME

Consider inventing a made-up "scientific name" for what you're afraid of, like Anxieta monstera if you are afraid of monsters, or Anxieta thunderstorma if thunder and lightning frighten you.

What could be a funny, pretend name for what makes you feel nervous?

LIFE IS ALWAYS A RICH AND STEADY TIME WHEN YOU ARE WAITING FOR SOMETHING TO HAPPEN OR TO HATCH.

— E. B. White
CHARLOTTE'S WEB

CATS & DOGS

TALKING WITHOUT WORDS

When we want to tell someone how we feel or what we'd like, we often use words.

"I feel happy," you might say.

Or: "I'd like a sandwich, please."

And: "Hey! Look at me!"

But not everyone uses words to say what they are feeling. People also use **nonverbal communication**, either sometimes or all the time.

Animals use nonverbal communication too.

If you have a pet cat or dog, chances are you've seen them stretch—probably many times a day! Hamsters, lizards, and other pets stretch too.

Cats are experts at finding a sunny spot on the floor, lying down with their legs straight out, and arching their backs in a slow, lazy stretch. Cats love to relax and nap in the sun—but they are also always on the lookout for danger. By keeping their muscles warmed up by stretching, they are ready to pounce.

Dogs stretch a lot too, sometimes dropping the front part of their body down and putting their backside up in the air. They also stretch to let people or other animals know when they are happy to see them or when they are feeling shy or if they want to become friends. They communicate by stretching in different ways.

Stretching is good for animals and for people. It increases the flow of blood in our bodies and keeps us from getting stiff after exercising or after sitting still for a long time, like during a car ride. Stretching first thing in the morning makes blood move more quickly to our muscles and brains and helps us feel more awake. For animals as well as humans, stretching can lead to a sense of well-being and calm.

What is **NONVERBAL COMMUNICATION?**

Nonverbal communication is a way to let someone know what you are thinking or feeling without using words. Pointing, changing what you are looking at, nodding, and turning your body away from someone or toward them are some ways we communicate nonverbally.

You can use nonverbal communication at the same time as you use words. If you are telling someone they did a good job, for example, you can clap your hands at the same time. This makes your praise even stronger. If you are feeling frustrated or angry and you slap your hand down on your lap, this shows the other person that you are having very strong feelings. Some people only use nonverbal communication to talk with others.

Next time you're with your pet—or when you're watching birds at a bird feeder or watching a movie about wild animals—quietly look at the way these creatures are holding and moving their bodies.

What are they saying to one another, without using words?

How do you think they are feeling?

What might they be saying to you?

What can you say to them, using only your body to communicate?

DID YOU KNOW?

Here are a few ways dogs stretch to tell us something:

- **Greeting stretch:** The dog leans forward and stretches their rear legs out behind them. Their ears look floppy and relaxed, their eyes squinty. Dogs never greet strangers or people they mistrust with the greeting stretch.

- **Nervous stretch:** When dogs stretch their ears straight backward and close to their heads, it means they are feeling shy or nervous.

- **Playful stretch:** When dogs wag their tails so hard that their bodies wiggle back and forth, and then crouch down into a squat, they are saying they want to play.

Practice
DOWNWARD DOG STRETCH

In yoga, the "downward dog" stretch is one of the first poses that is taught. It not only calms us down but gets blood flowing to the brain, making us feel alert and focused.

1. First get down on your hands and knees on a soft patch of grass outside or on a yoga mat indoors. Keep your back straight.

2. Then curl your toes under, straighten your knees, and lift your bottom up into the air.

3. Keep your head between your arms for a few seconds. When you are done, lower your knees to the mat.

If you have trouble doing this pose, you can do it your own way. For example, you could stretch your arms out toward a table or a fence and bend over as far as feels comfortable to you.

I AM PERFECTLY ME

For the next few seconds, picture yourself hiking up a mountain path. Even if you've never gone on a hike like that, just try to imagine it in your mind.

Let's pretend it's a sunny day in late spring—not too warm, not too cold. It's an easy climb, not steep at all. You walk slowly and steadily, and the path rises in front of you, like it's gently pulling you higher and higher toward the top of the mountain. There are trees on either side of you, tall pines whose fallen needles create a thick carpet under your feet. Ferns grow around the bases of the tree trunks.

DID YOU KNOW?
WATERFALLS MAKE US HAPPY

Being near waterfalls makes people feel happy. Scientists explain that **negative ions** are created when wind and water break air molecules apart. Negative ions are invisible, and we breathe them in at the beach, on mountain walks, and after it rains. They help release **serotonin**, a chemical in our brains that makes us feel happy. Next time it rains, open a window or go outside. Take a walk when the storm passes, breathe in those negative ions, and let them fill you up with happiness!

The path weaves around a bend, bringing a waterfall into sight. You stand still for a few minutes, just watching water cascade into the pool below. A dragonfly, shiny with a metallic blue-and-yellow body and wings, shimmers and flits ahead of you.

Standing there, you suddenly feel aware of all the patterns and shapes you see, and your heart feels light, like it's been filled up like a helium balloon. The **symmetrical** body of the dragonfly. The way the tiniest leaves of the ferns look like miniatures of the whole plant. The jagged zigzag shape of nearby mountain peaks. The cracks in the rock around the waterfall, splintered like lightning. Gray-green moss polka-dotting the boulders along the edge of the path.

You take a deep breath in, and you let it out. It feels good to notice these things. They seem . . . well . . . perfect!

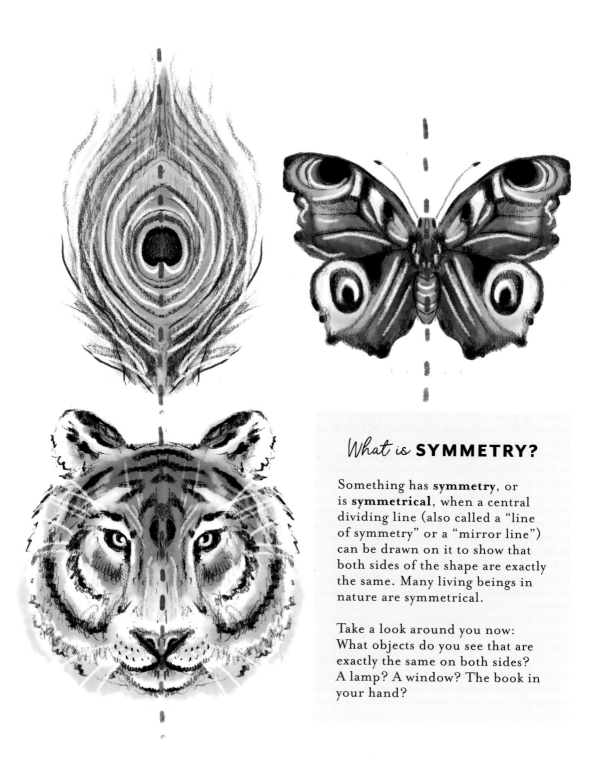

What is SYMMETRY?

Something has **symmetry**, or is **symmetrical**, when a central dividing line (also called a "line of symmetry" or a "mirror line") can be drawn on it to show that both sides of the shape are exactly the same. Many living beings in nature are symmetrical.

Take a look around you now: What objects do you see that are exactly the same on both sides? A lamp? A window? The book in your hand?

THAT'S THE WHOLE SECRET OF MEDITATION,
THAT YOU BECOME THE WATCHER.

— Osho
THE PATH OF MEDITATION

SPIRALS

EMBRACING A GROWTH MINDSET

A spiral is one of the most common shapes in nature. Massive things like hurricanes are spiral shaped; so are tiny things like fingerprints. Blow out a candle, and smoke will spiral up toward the ceiling. Visit the reptile house at the zoo and see the snakes, their bodies coiled into perfect spirals. Spirals are everywhere!

Spirals can remind us that things are always moving and changing. The good and bad parts of our lives shift. A hard day is followed by a happier one. Sometimes we are laughing one minute but then feel sad the next. Things shift and evolve. Paths can take lots of twists and turns. Things spin, and then they settle down again.

All through human history, people have tried to understand what spirals mean. People who lived long, long ago closely followed the phases of the moon, the seasons, and other cycles in nature to tell time and to plan their crops and harvests. And thousands of years before humans began to write, ancient people painted and drew spirals on walls and pottery and in their other artwork.

If spirals appear so often in the natural world—much more than shapes with straight lines, like squares—might Earth be trying to tell us something special through them?

What could that be?

What do you think?

What do spirals tell us about life?

What are **SPIRALS?**

Spirals are special curves that start at a point, then go around the point, curving farther and farther away.

It can be helpful, when you are feeling down, to remember that what you're feeling now is not what you will always feel. *Now isn't forever.* Tracing the spiral can remind you to pay attention to what is happening *right now* but also to be aware that life keeps moving and changing. It's not helpful to look behind at where you have been; instead, just focus on where you are, moving forward and growing every day.

Like the clouds up in the sky, your feelings come and go. They might block out the sun for a time, but then they pass. They might grow dark and stormy, but then they clear.

You're not stuck; things change.

FIXED VS. GROWTH MINDSET
Two Ways of Thinking

Some people have what's called a "fixed mindset." They think that if they are struggling now or are not very good at something now, that's the way it always will be. They feel stuck, and they often feel unhappy.

The opposite way of thinking is to have a "growth mindset." People who think this way believe that skills can be practiced and improved and that things can get better.

Why does this matter? Well, when we have a growth mindset, we know that we can change and get better and that life can change and get better. We know that we can learn from our mistakes and improve. We know that if we feel bad today, we might feel good tomorrow.

People with a growth mindset believe that change is possible and give themselves more chances to be happy and learn new things.

Creating
A SPIRAL

Go outside and collect stones, acorns, pine cones, leaves, dandelions, and sticks—collect a variety of things from nature, without damaging any living things or habitats. Arrange these things into a spiral shape on the ground or on a table.

While you arrange your spiral, think about each item you touch. *Was it always in the form it is now? Might a rock have broken off from a large boulder? Didn't a dandelion start as a seed? How have these things changed? Are they still changing?*

The leaf in your hand was once a tiny bud. Acorns begin life as flowers. Pine cones develop from tiny pollen grains.

Your life, too, changes and evolves over time.

When you feel like you are locked in a hard time, and you are focused on what happened before or what might happen later, imagine yourself spiraling away from a central point, and know that things do change. Things can get better. Embrace a growth mindset!

TRACING A SPIRAL

Next time you are feeling rushed or nervous, come back to this page and slowly trace your finger around the picture of a spiral. Focus on the smooth paper under your fingertip and the way your arm moves in circles as you follow the curve.

SHAPES

CELEBRATING DIFFERENCE

What's your favorite color?

If your answer is "blue," does that mean that blue is the *best* color? The most beautiful? That every other color—green, gold, pink, yellow, red—isn't as nice?

Of course not!

Nature is full of colors, shapes, smells, tastes, and other gifts. There's no right answer, no "best" when we are looking at the wonder of all that is alive.

And there is no best shape. Although spirals are amazing, they, of course, are not the only shape we see repeated in nature. Hexagons, branching patterns, and circles are a few more.

Honeybees create perfect **hexagons** when they make their hives.

Look up high into a tree and see how each limb **branches off** into tiny shoots.

Circles, including the half circle of a rainbow, are also all around us.

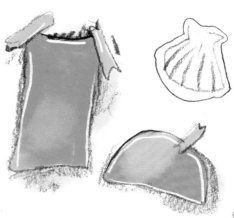

Does a circle compare itself to a hexagon and feel like it's somehow not as good?

Does pink compare itself with green and feel bad about the way it looks?

Does a tree limb on an old oak tree wonder why a seashell has spiral shapes instead of branching ones?

Nope!

And the same is true for all of us. We are all different. We use different pronouns to describe ourselves. We have different haircuts.

We like different music and flavors of ice cream. And different things make us laugh and cry.

Look around you now or go look out a window.

What hexagons, branches, or circles do *you* see?

Which shape is most beautiful to you?

What do you like about it?

What is a **HEXAGON?**

A **hexagon** is a six-sided, six-cornered shape. It gets its name from the Greek *hex*, meaning "six," and *gonia*, meaning "corner."

Remember the dragonfly you saw when you went on that imaginary hike earlier in this book? If you were to look very closely at its eyes, you'd find that they are made up of 30,000 tiny lenses, and each one is the shape of a hexagon. Snowflakes are also hexagons. You can see hexagons, too, on a turtle's shell. A huge cloud formation at the north pole of Saturn is also—you guessed it—a hexagon!

What is a **LENS?**

The **lens** is the clear part of the eye behind the **iris** (the colored part of the eye). The lens—in humans, dragonflies, jellyfish, goats, and other beings who can see—allows the eye to focus on things that are both very close and very far away.

When people talk about hexagons in nature, the first example they usually give is honeycombs—those six-sided cells that hold the queen honeybee's eggs and store honey.

But *how* and *why* do bees create the honeycombs in that shape? We aren't sure. We do know that the cells begin as circles, but then, some scientists say, the bees use heat from their bodies to melt the wax into perfect hexagons.

Bees are smart: By making hexagons in their combs, they create the most sturdy and largest possible number of storage units, using the least amount of wax. You see, if they made them in circle shapes, there would be gaps between cells, wasting wax and wasting space.

What is a BRANCHING PATTERN?

A seed sprouts, and after growing taller and stronger, the plant splits into **branches**. Each of these again splits into new branches. Branches help carry air, food, water, and gases to and from the deepest tissues in living things.

The branching of roots allows trees and other plants to reach out deep or far into the soil below them or up high into the sky so they can bring water and sunlight and food to their cores.

Human bodies do the same kind of thing. Blood vessels branch out from our hearts, moving blood around the body. They branch off, getting smaller the farther they are from the heart. Blood vessels called **arteries** carry blood out of the heart; ones called **veins** return blood to the heart.

The moon, rings in a tree stump, water droplets, and oranges are just a few circle-shaped things we commonly see.

Looking at curving, circular shapes, scientists tell us, makes us feel cozy and safe. They think this is true because, as human beings **evolved**, sharp and pointy things, like jagged rocks or pointy animal horns, were signs of danger. (Remember how our fears try to protect us?)

But softly curving things, like rounded doorways or fruit hanging from a tree or a pudgy little puppy, feel safe and invite us to come near.

What can you think of that's round and that people think of as a "happy" thing?

A beachball?

A balloon?

A lollipop?

A trampoline?

A bike wheel?

What else can you think of that's round and that makes people feel happy?

What is EVOLUTION?

Living things **evolve**, or change, over time. (This is also called "adaptation.") Plants, animals, and human beings evolve so that they will not only *survive* in a certain place but *thrive*.

Polar bears, for example, evolved from brown bears.

Why might bears survive and thrive better in snowy, icy habitats with white fur rather than brown?

COLLECT NATURAL TREASURES

What shape do you like best? Spirals? Hexagons? Branching patterns? Circles?

Collect a few treasures that are that shape.

If you like branching patterns, for instance, pick up a leaf that's fallen below a tree and trace the branching pattern of the veins. Those veins, branching up from the leaf's stem, carry water and food through the leaf, just like your vessels and arteries carry blood through your body to keep you healthy.

WHAT WOULD IT FEEL LIKE TO BE PART OF A FAMILY
THAT INCLUDES BIRCHES AND BEAVERS AND BUTTERFLIES?
WE'D BE LESS LONELY. WE'D FEEL LIKE WE BELONGED.
WE'D BE SMARTER.

— *Robin Wall Kimmerer*
"NATURE NEEDS A NEW PRONOUN"

SPOTS & STRIPES

STANDING OUT AND BLENDING IN

They're interesting and beautiful to look at, but have you ever wondered *why* zebras have stripes or *why* giraffes have spots?

And what does that have to do with *you*?

As you read in the last chapter, living things evolve, or change, over time so they can survive and thrive in a certain place. (Remember how brown bears *evolved* to match snowy environments?)

Spotted and striped creatures evolved to best match their habitats. Their camouflage keeps them safe from predators, but it does even more.

Until recently, for example, scientists thought a zebra's stripes were there just to confuse predators. When zebras are clustered together with their jarring, over-lapping stripes, the lions and hyenas who might attack seem to get confused. They seem to wonder where one zebra stops and another starts, so they leave them alone.

But now biologists think zebras' stripes are really there to confuse much tinier creatures: flies. Fly bites can infect zebras with disease, and unlike others in their genus such as horses, zebras don't have long, swishy tails to bat away bugs. Instead, zebras evolved to have stripes to confuse disease-carrying flies, who have trouble seeing them properly. Researchers have learned that flies, as they get ready to land on zebras' backs and bite them, get mixed up by the black-and-white jumble of stripes and fly away.

Some spots and stripes do more than serve as camouflage. While giraffes' spots help them blend in with their yellow-and-brown home, the African savanna, those spots are also like a built-in air-conditioning system. When humans get hot, we sweat; giraffes, however, don't. Instead, they pump hot blood under their dark spots (called "thermal windows"), and heat escapes from their bodies that way. Also, no two giraffes have the same pattern of spots, and scientists who study them say that giraffes recognize one another because of the pattern of their spots.

What is **CAMOUFLAGE?**

Camouflage is when living beings blend in with their surroundings to find food or to protect themselves. Two types of camouflage are:

- **Concealing camouflage**:
  Conceal means "hide." Concealing camouflage is when living creatures' coloring matches the backdrop of where they live. (Remember that white polar bear in the snow? Or think about brown owls living in trees whose bark is the same color and has similar patterns as the owls' feathers!)

- **Deceptive camouflage**:
  Deceptive means "false" or "disguised." Deceptive camouflage is when patterns on plants' leaves or animals' skin hide their outline against their background. Some insects, including walking sticks and katydids (also known as leaf bugs), camouflage themselves by looking like a leaf or twig, making it very hard for predators to see them.

Which is more interesting: the black-and-white spots on a panda or the colorful stripes of an angel fish? If you answered, "Neither," you're right!

Beauty, as the old saying goes, is in the eye of the beholder. In other words, different people find different things beautiful.

Zebras and pandas with their black-and-white markings, giraffes and cheetahs with their brown-and-tan spots, bright red cardinals and dart frogs, gray elephants and manatees—they are all interesting and beautiful, each in their own way.

You have your own look and way of being in the world too!

Sometimes the way you look makes you blend in, and sometimes it might make you feel like you "stick out."

FITTING IN ·AND·
STANDING OUT

Sometimes you will want to fit in. Sometimes you won't. Sometimes you will feel like you are part of a herd. Sometimes you will feel alone.

Everyone feels these ways sometimes. Make a list of all the ways you fit in with people around you and ways that you stand out. What differences are you proud of? What do you wish you could change? Reflect on when you want to camouflage yourself to blend in and when you purposely try to stand out.

Remember, you being exactly the way you are in this moment helps make the whole world more beautiful. Embrace your uniqueness! You are wonderful just the way you are.

ALL THAT THE SUN SHINES ON IS BEAUTIFUL,
SO LONG AS IT IS WILD.

— John Muir

I AM IN FLOW

When people say they're "in flow," they mean they are totally focused on what they are doing. Some people call it "being in the zone." When we're in flow, we aren't thinking about what happened yesterday or what might happen tomorrow: we are fully into whatever we're doing *right now*.

Maybe you feel this way when you are reading a good book. The characters and setting capture your attention and feel so real to you that, when someone calls your name, you feel like you have actually been somewhere else. You don't know whether you've been reading for ten minutes—or ten hours! Or maybe it's when you are painting or coding or writing a poem or playing a musical instrument.

Or maybe it happens when you are playing sports, your legs and arms and muscles working hard, and without even thinking about it, everything feels easy—and you score! When the final bell or buzzer sounds, you can't believe the game is over. Time has zoomed by.

When we're in flow, we are focused. We feel happy. And time seems like it has sped up. Even if we are working or thinking hard, everything feels more like play. When you are in flow, you may have a strong and strange feeling that you might say is thankfulness.

When have you lost track of time doing something you love to do? Think about this time you were in flow.

A lot of things in nature flow. Lava boils in and then flows out of volcanoes. Water flows in streams and rivers and oceans. Sap flows sweetly inside trees. These things flow without thinking about it, without trying. They just *are*.

WHEN YOU DO THINGS FROM YOUR SOUL, YOU FEEL A RIVER MOVING IN YOU, A JOY.

— *Rumi*

LAVA

INVESTIGATING STRONG FEELINGS

Scientists who study volcanoes are called volcanologists. **Volcanologists** work to understand how and why volcanoes erupt. They do this so they can help predict future eruptions.

Sometimes our feelings feel as boiling hot as lava. Someone is unkind to us or misunderstands us or takes something that belongs to us, and—*BOOM!*—an eruption happens deep inside us. Anger, fear, jealousy—these feelings can bubble under the surface in us. And just like with hot lava, we can't throw a bucket of water over them and cool them. Ignoring them sometimes just makes them burn more hotly.

Our Earth has about 1,500 active volcanoes, but did you know there are volcanoes on other planets, too, including Mercury, Venus, and Mars? On Earth, most volcanoes are in countries found near the Pacific Ocean.

RING OF FIRE

Wherever they are in the universe, volcanoes hold very hot liquid called **magma**. You might have seen pictures of it, glowing orange inside a volcano. When a volcano erupts, this magma flows out of the volcano and is then called **lava**.

Lava can be as hot as 2,200 degrees Fahrenheit! (If you have ever had a very hot cup of cocoa, it was probably about 100 degrees, so lava is more than twenty times hotter than that!) When lava cools and hardens, it becomes **igneous rock**. Igneous comes from a Latin word, *ignis*, that means "fire."

Some volcanic eruptions have created islands in the ocean. The islands that make up the state of Hawaii, for example, were formed by volcanoes. The lava flows, layers over itself, cools, and then builds up to create land.

FUN FACT

The largest volcano in our solar system is on Mars. Named "Olympus Mons," it is about 16 miles high and stretches across an area about the size of the state of Arizona!

Interview
YOUR FEELINGS

One way to cool your temper or weaken your fears is to pretend you're a volcanologist studying an active volcano. Next time you feel an eruption of anger or sadness or jealousy starting to bubble up inside you, grab a piece of paper and a pencil and play the following game.

First, introduce yourself to your feeling [we'll start with Anger]:

"Hello, Anger! I feel that you might be getting ready to erupt. I'm here to ask you a few questions."

Jot down the answers as you ask your difficult feeling these things:

- Can you tell me, please, on a scale of 1 to 10 (with 10 being strongest) how large an eruption might occur?

- What happened that made you get so strong all of a sudden?
- Has this happened before?
- When?
- What was that eruption like?
- What new landscapes might this eruption create if it happens?
- What damage might this eruption cause to people around me?
- Is there anything that happened last time that we could avoid this time?
- Is there anything that might cool this flow of lava?

At the end of your interview, you could say, "Thank you, Anger, for your time. It was interesting to get to know you better."

Sometimes just naming a boiling hot or painful feeling calms it down a little and helps prevent an explosive eruption.

WATER

KEEPING HYDRATED

The surface of our Earth is more than 70 percent water, and water is what makes all life possible for every plant, animal, insect, and everything else!

Water is in all living things too: Our bodies are actually mostly water! A baby is almost 80 percent water; older folks' bodies are more than 50 percent water. Because our bodies are mostly water, keeping your body **hydrated** is an important way to stay healthy and happy. (**To hydrate** means "to add water.") For most kids, drinking eight or nine cups of water per day is the right amount. (You can use a measuring cup when you first start paying attention to how much water you're drinking.)

Water is the part of the blood that brings nutrients to our cells. Water helps waste leave our bodies. And it helps us stay the right temperature—not too hot and not too cold.

Keeping hydrated has many other benefits too. Kids who are well hydrated do better on tests and quizzes. People who are hydrated experience less depression and anxiety. They also feel more energized and more awake.

Taking good care of yourself by drinking enough water can make you feel calmer and have more energy. You deserve to have these good feelings, and drinking water can help.

Turn on the faucet, let water flow into a glass, and fill yourself up!

PEACE IS ALWAYS BEAUTIFUL.

— *Walt Whitman*
"THE SLEEPERS"

WATER FUN FACTS

- The water we drink has been around since Earth was formed millions of years ago. When you drink a glass of water, you could be drinking water that was once drunk by dinosaurs, the first humans, and heroes like Harriet Tubman and Gandhi.
- Almost 97 percent of the water on Earth is salty and not usable by most living things, except special ones such as mangrove trees.
- About 75 percent of the human brain is water!
- A living tree is 75 percent—you guessed it!—water.

OTHER WAYS TO ENJOY WATER

SKIPPING STONES

Next time you are near a pond, lake, or other calm body of water, try skipping stones. Also called "skimming stones," the idea is to throw a smooth, flat stone or pebble the way you throw a Frisbee, hard and with a flick of your wrist, so it bounces over the surface of the water.

But how can rocks not sink when you skim them?

In this book's "Wingspans" chapter, you learned that birds resist the force of gravity by using lift force. The same is true when a rock skips over water. Just like how birds create lift by keeping the front part of their wings higher than the back, when we skip stones, the angle above the water's surface (as well as its spin rate and speed) keeps it from sinking down into the water.

FLOATING YOUR WORRIES AWAY

Have you ever floated on your back or on an inflatable mattress in a lake or swimming pool? How do you feel when you stare up at the sky or when you close your eyes and experience the movement of the water? Floating on water, whether it's inside or outside, can help you feel calmer, more creative, and less stressed out. Being in or on the water can even help your body recover after being injured or ill.

Even if you don't live by a lake or pool, you can practice this kind of relaxation exercise. Just let your body relax in the bathtub or lie down on your bed and imagine yourself floating on gentle waves.

Close your eyes, pay attention to your breathing as you gently breathe in and out, and let your worries drift away.

FOR A LONG TIME, THEY LOOKED AT THE RIVER BENEATH THEM, SAYING NOTHING, AND THE RIVER SAID NOTHING TOO, FOR IT FELT VERY QUIET AND PEACEFUL ON THIS SUMMER AFTERNOON.

— A. A. Milne
THE HOUSE AT POOH CORNER

SAP

LETTING GO

Have you ever tasted real maple syrup? Maybe you've poured it on a big pile of pancakes, the golden-brown syrup sticky and delicious. Did you ever wonder where it comes from?

Like blood in our bodies, sap is a tree's "blood." While our blood carries nutrients and minerals throughout our bodies, sap does the same for trees. Maples are the trees that contain the sap that can be made into the syrup we love at breakfast.

It takes about 40 gallons of tree sap to make just one gallon of syrup. And it all just kind of flows, thanks to changing temperatures.

When the wood in the tree rises above freezing, it causes some pressure in the tree and makes the sap flow. It flows out of a hole drilled into the tree or through a broken branch. Again, sap is like our blood, and it flows out where there is a "cut." If temperatures fall below freezing, sap is sucked back into trees, and they hold their sap and save up energy. When the temperatures rise again, sap will flow out of the tree again. Many maple trees have been "tapped" for syrup every year for more than a hundred years! After it flows from the tree, the sap must be boiled right away to make syrup. In the United States, between 3 and 4 million gallons of syrup are made every year.

NO NEED TO HURRY. NO NEED TO SPARKLE.
NO NEED TO BE ANYBODY BUT ONESELF.

— *Virginia Woolf*
"A ROOM OF ONE'S OWN"

One story about the discovery of maple syrup is that an Indigenous leader of the Iroquois, named Chief Woksis, threw his tomahawk—an axe-like tool—at a maple tree on a cold spring day. The next day, the sun warmed the sap inside the tree, and from the hole where the tomahawk had struck the tree, sap flowed out. That hidden, delicious surprise was there all along but just needed a way to make its way out.

TWO KINDS OF SAP

- **Xylem** carries water and minerals from the bottom of the tree to its leaves at the top, feeding it to help it grow. Maple syrup is made from xylem.
- **Phloem** carries the sugars produced by the leaves at the top of the tree down to the trunk to feed the tree.

Sometimes our feelings are as hidden as sap inside a maple tree. Maybe we hold on to a good memory, and when we think about it, it's as though the warm sun is shining down on us. Other times we hold on to memories that hurt when we think about them. We wish we could release them and let them flow out of us, far away.

Locking painful feelings up inside, like frozen sap in a tree, isn't good for our health or happiness. It can give us stomachaches or make other parts of our bodies feel uncomfortable. To begin letting such feelings go, releasing them and letting them flow like sap on a warm day, you can do some of these things:

Repeat a helpful mantra, like "I can let this go" or "I can forgive" or "I am moving forward."
- Talk to a trusted adult about your feelings.
- Shout into a pillow.
- Make a "gratitude list" of all the things that are good.
- Go on a walk and ask Nature to be your helpful teacher and guide, showing you the way to let go.
- Have a good cry.

HAVE A GOOD CRY

Did you know that our eyes make a few different kinds of tears? Some, called **reflex tears** and **continuous tears**, help clear out dust, smoke, and other harmful things from our eyes.

But when we cry—whether it's because you're excited, angry, sad, or laughing really hard—our tears are different. Called emotional tears, this type of tear flushes toxins, or harmful chemicals, out of our bodies and releases feel-good chemicals inside of us that help us feel better. Sometimes people who feel like they could use a "good cry" watch sad movies or listen to sad music to stir up those feelings and flush out their systems. They know that letting their tears flow is one way to feel a lot better.

Next time you feel that tight feeling in your throat or a flood of emotion stirring around inside of you, open yourself up to a good cry.

- Take a few deep breaths and settle down into paying attention as you breathe in and out.
- Imagine for a few moments that you are a maple tree in the springtime.
- Close your eyes and picture what that would feel like.
- Feel the sun shining on you, helping you feel relaxed, warming your bark.
- After a winter of holding in your sap, begin to let it flow.
- Imagine that the things that worry you or make you feel stressed are in that sap.
- Imagine, too, that someone is collecting your tears in a bucket. Your fears, your bad memories, the things that hold you down, words people said that hurt your feelings—these painful thoughts are dripping—*tap, tap, tapping*—into the bucket beside you. They will fill the bucket and be taken away to be warmed over a fire. Heated up, those problems and hard feelings and disappointments will change. They will boil and thicken and become something sweet and good.

Let yourself feel what you're feeling.

Let yourself have a good cry.

I CAN Grow AND Change

SEASONS

KNOWING THAT NOW ISN'T FOREVER

There are four seasons every year: spring, summer, fall (also called "autumn"), and winter. Each season lasts for three months—at least, officially, on the calendar.

Seasons are caused by Earth's ever-changing relationship to the sun. Earth travels around the sun once every 365 days (365 days = 1 year). Over the course of the year, the amount of sunlight each spot on the planet gets each day changes, causing the seasons.

What's your favorite season?

Why do you love it?

People talk about the "seasons" in their lives too. When someone is feeling homesick or lonely, they might say they are in a sad season or even describe this hard time as "winter" (even if it's July in Florida!). When we're starting a new adventure and feeling full of hope, we might describe that season in our lives as "spring," when new life is popping up and we feel a burst of energy.

Some people describe the parts of human life—from birth to very old age—as seasons too. A child can be described as being in the "spring of life," while an elderly person is sometimes said to be in the "autumn" or "winter" of their life, a time when not much is new or growing, when the trees are bare and the sky gray.

Imagine yourself as an old person, in the "fall" or "winter" of your life.

What do you want to remember about what it feels like to be you, now, at your younger age?

What do you see, experience, or appreciate right now that you want to keep seeing and enjoying when you're older?

Create a
SEASON NOTEBOOK

In this chapter, we are going to try something new!

We are going to create a nature notebook for the seasons. Find a spiral notebook or sketch pad or even just a stack of scrap paper. You can be as plain or fancy as you like, decorating the cover or putting pages in a folder or just slipping it all into the back of this book.

Your season notebook will have, as you might guess, four parts—one for each season. In the notebook, you can draw or paint; glue in leaves, petals, and sticks; or just write about what you see. The important thing is to be on the lookout in each season, seeing clues about what nature is telling you about the time of year you are in *right now*.

Whenever you use your nature notebook, you'll begin by looking out a window or going outdoors.

YOU CAN ASK YOURSELF:

- What do I see?
- What do the trees tell me about the season I'm in?
- What do the grass, flowers, and other plants tell me about this season?
- How much light is in the sky in this season? Does it look different than it did a few weeks or months ago?
- What birds or other creatures do I see? What can I learn about this season from them?
- Do my feelings match this season? In what ways do I feel the same as or different from what I see in the trees, sky, and creatures of this season?

Most of all, look at nature with a beginner's mind and record what you see.

TAKE NOTE

- Why is that pebble smooth? What made it that way? Was it always that size and shape?
- Why is that stick so easy to break?
- Why are those flowers the color and shape they are?
- What time of day is the brightest? When is the sun going down?
- Does the air smell the same as it did a few months ago? Do I smell any trees or flowers? Does the air smell different now, just after it has snowed or rained?
- Is that plant young or old? How will it change from the way it is now?

FOLLOWING SEASONS

Each season has different gifts and surprises. Depending on where you live, here are some things to pay special attention to in the four seasons:

WINTER

In the winter, some animals **hibernate**, or "nap," in caves or other safe places until warmer weather comes again. Other creatures, including insects, fish, and birds, **migrate** in the winter. This means they travel to other parts of the world to escape the cold.

What animals or birds do you see in the winter where you live?

Do any birds visit your area from far away?

Winter is a time when the ground "lies fallow." This means it rests and doesn't grow any plants. It is good for the soil to rest.

Winter can be a time for people to be quiet, rest, and lie fallow too.

SPRING

In the spring, new life appears.

In your nature notebook, record the first day you see new plant life coming up outside, little seedlings or new flowers bursting through the soil. Write down and record the day when you first see buds on the tree branches.

How do they change from day to day?

Does your mood change, or do you notice any new feelings when you start seeing tulips peeking up through the dirt or hearing birds sing?

SUMMER

Summer can be a time for exploration. You might have more free time, time to collect and paint rocks or skim stones (see the "Water" chapter in this book), or to go on walks in the woods or a beach, looking for fish skeletons, rocks, crab claws, shells, pine cones, and more.

You can also plant a garden in the summertime, watching flowers or vegetables sprout and grow.

What's something you do in the summer that you don't do at other times of year?

How does it make you feel?

What is being planted in you?

FALL

In the fall, go on a walk at a park or in the woods and look for signs of animal life, including tracks, chewed bark on trees, and nests.

You can create leaf art by collecting fallen leaves and then arranging them into different shapes in your notebook.

What are the birds and animals doing to prepare for winter?

What are you doing to get ready for a colder, less colorful time of year?

GREETING THE EARTH

In the ancient Indian language of Sanskrit, one way to say hello is to use a simple word: "Namaste" (*NAHM-uh-stay*). One translation of this greeting is "The light in me sees the light in you."

As you go out into the world with your nature notebook, consider beginning your investigations by greeting the earth with this word as you look for the life and the light in all you see.

"GO OUTSIDE, OFTEN, SOMETIMES IN WILD PLACES.
BRING FRIENDS OR NOT. BREATHE."

— Florence Williams
"THE NATURE FIX"

I CAN ASK, "WHAT IS?" INSTEAD OF "WHAT IF?"

Everyone needs to find calm sometimes. We *all* have fears and worries, and this book doesn't tell you *not* to worry or *not* to have painful or uncomfortable feelings. Instead, it reminds you of a few things that can help you feel better when you do.

One is that you can be curious about your fears or worries, observing them like a scientist. Remember that like Wilbur's best friend, Charlotte, our worries are strange and protective friends. They want to keep us safe. We can watch them, learn about them, and listen to what they are trying to tell us. And we can learn to let them go.

Another way to calm down when your worries feel like too much is to pay attention to the present moment and focus on "what is" rather than "what if." Just be right where you are, focused on *right now*, like a spider carefully spinning a web or a dandelion seed blowing in the wind or a cat lying in the sun. They aren't thinking about yesterday or tomorrow. They are present, right here and right now.

For example, if you are worried about starting at a new school, you might tend to ask questions or think thoughts like these:

What if I don't make any friends?

What if the teachers are harder than the ones I had at my old school?

What if I don't make the basketball team?

These are very understandable fears, but if they stick around too long, they can become a problem. They might give you a stomachache or keep you from sleeping well or make it hard to have fun reading or drawing or being with friends. When unhelpful thoughts hang around too long, practice looking at "what is" instead of "what if?"

Practice
WHAT IS

To begin, sit, stand, or lie down in a quiet place.

Pay attention to your breath.

Breathe in through your nose, letting your lungs fill with air. Breathe out through your mouth and let those out-breaths be even longer than your in-breaths. You can make sounds on your out-breaths too. Try quietly drawing out the word "hope" or "home" with your out-breath.

Once your breathing has settled down, think about what is. To do this, look around—wherever you are. If you're indoors, look out a window.

Ask yourself:

What do I see that has roots?

What do I see that stretches?

What designs and colors and patterns do I see?

What flows?

What season is it?

Try to look with a beginner's mind at everything you can see, right here, right now.

You can even thank your fears for trying to help you, but also let them know that they can stop sounding the alarm. You can let them know you'll be all right, right where you are.

JENNIFER GRANT is the award-winning author of picture books for children and books for adults. Her books include *Maybe God Is Like That Too*, *Maybe I Can Love My Neighbor Too*, and *Dimming the Day*. Grant's work has appeared in *Woman's Day*, *Chicago Parent*, *Patheos*, and *Chicago Tribune*. Grant holds a master's degree in English literature with concentrations in creative writing and critical theory from Southern Methodist University in Dallas. A lifelong Episcopalian and mother of four, she lives in Chicago with her husband.

ERIN BROWN is a Northern Irish illustrator who lives on the beautiful island of Jersey. She combines her love for hand-drawn lines with the flexibility of adding color digitally. When she's not working, she can be found exploring the forests and cliff paths of Jersey or down at the seashore.